BREAK THROUGH YOUR HIRING & RETENTION BARRIERS

HOW SUCCESSFUL LEADERS ATTRACT AND KEEP THE RIGHT EMPLOYEES

HOLLY ROUILLARD JOHNSON

Bonus Offer

Thank you for purchasing your copy of *Break Through Your Hiring & Retention Barriers*. Although I highly recommend reading the book, I also understand we live in a fast world where video and audio options are also appreciated.

For this reason, I have created an on-line course where I cover this book in video, which can also be listened to in your car or on your phone in audio. Here, I share the key elements of this book and some additional insights.

To access this, please scan the QR code below:

Publishing and Design:

EP♦C AUTHOR
P U B L I S H I N G

Ordering Information: Exclusive discounts for quantity purchases.

Contact: 561-601-9871 | info@epicauthor.com | EpicAuthor.com

First Edition

Table Of Contents

Foreword

WHEN HOLLY ASKED ME to write the Foreword for *Break Through Your Hiring & Retention Barriers,* I jumped at the chance to contribute. I had recently read one of her other books, *How to Make Feeling Good Your Priority,* which shed light on both her personal and professional approach to life, work, and helping others achieve their goals. This book provides the kind of clarity everyone can use to address and improve their hiring and retention challenges during these difficult times.

Unemployment is at record lows, and Covid changed how so many of us work -- choosing from home over going to an office. Leadership in all sectors of our economy is waning, and there is a wave of "quiet quitting," and more, putting more pressure on business owners, CEOs and organization leaders across all industries and government sectors.

Arguably, this is the most challenging period in hiring and retention I've seen in my more than 30-year career, making *Break Through Your Hiring & Retention Barriers* perfectly timed.

My name is Scott Shafer, and I am the chief executive officer of Absolute Performance, Inc., a global technology company based in Broomfield, Colorado that has grown from $1 million in annual revenue in 2014 to more than $50 million in 2023 and 300 employees, with a less than 3% annual attrition rate. This kind of retention is something I have been able to accomplish and carry over from other corporate positions and ventures. This includes building another technology and business process outsourcing company that started as a handshake in a Detroit Starbucks to more than 1,500 people in three years. In addition, I have also been blessed to work with a group of wicked smart parents to build a charter school that has been ranked as a Top 100 U.S. high school every year for more than 15 years.

This hiring and retention success is something you can achieve. My colleagues and I have done it using the principles laid out in this book.

What Holly lays out in the ensuing pages provides a blueprint for successfully hiring and retaining people, who in turn take care of your customers, resulting in the growth and profitability of your business. It's so simple, yet so overlooked, and an exacting overlay of my other ventures.

The first step in achieving successfully hiring and retention is with YOU...where are you taking your company? What is your vision, mission, and strategies? Are you passionate and genuinely inspired to help grow your employees' skill sets that lead to higher level of customer and supplier satisfaction? Holly lays out a personal roadmap for you and your company or business to begin driving results.

By following this personal roadmap, you can easily apply the principles Holly lays out in *Breaking Through Your Hiring & Retention Barriers* and achieve success.

Now, about hiring and retention.

A common theme I hear for employee attrition is money and benefits.

There's a scene in one of my favorite movies where the bad guys are digging frantically for a treasure. The good guys are watching, and laughing, from a hill not far away lamenting "they're digging in the wrong place!"

Money and benefits are a factor in employee hiring and retention for sure, but not the only factor. It's like digging in the wrong place. There is no "one thing" or treasure to resolve your challenges. In this book Holly cites a study of the top 16 reasons for employee attrition, and only one (1) has to do with money...the rest are about YOU!

What I've learned from Holly over the years, and so well-articulated in this book, is how attract, hire, and retain the right people in creating an energizing environment. In turn, these engaged employees energize your customers, so they stay loyal and end up buying more, which enables your business to grow in a more profitable direction.

Congratulations on taking the first, and most important step toward hiring and retaining great people -- letting Holly help you.

Scott Shafer, CEO
Absolute Performance, Inc.

Introduction

IF YOU'RE A CHIEF EXECUTIVE OFFICER (CEO) or business owner struggling to attract and keep the employees that matter, I understand your frustration. Prompted by three decades of my own experiences managing two public relations (PR) and marketing firms and working with businesses—from small hotels and restaurants to a large national health insurance company—I have personally witnessed how having a great team makes a great company. I have seen how one wrong hire can erode a company's culture and destroy a business.

My own personal collision course happened when I ran a seven-figure marketing, PR, and design firm, humming along with an enviable client list and a key director whom everyone trusted and admired. Then, one day, she quit. I was dumbfounded. Not only was she dependable and respected, but she was also the glue that kept our firm together. And it couldn't have come at a worse time. We were maxed out on client work and needed *someone* in the door fast.

Guess what we got—someone. This someone eroded our company culture and nearly destroyed our company.

So how can one person do this? I allowed it. I lost focus on our vision, our mission, and, most importantly, the work I truly loved.

Stressed out, hating my job, feeling like all I did was manage over-head and put out fires, I couldn't see the forest through the trees. Sound familiar? Do you look at your business and your responsibilities and wonder how one day you're doing what you love and the next day doing everything in your power just to hang on?

You're not alone. Based on hundreds of hours of research, hiring and retention are the #1 frustrations among business owners and CEOs, commanding up to 40 percent of your time EVERY DAY, and costing you tens, if not hundreds, of thousands of dollars.

I'm here to tell you there is a light at the end of your tunnel—and it's not an oncoming train. It's a simple, three-step process used by successful business owners, CEOs, and organization leaders that can—and will—take you from where you are to where you want to be—able to attract and keep the employees who matter.

———

CHAPTER ONE

Getting Started

FIRST, I'd like to share a little story with you about one of my favorite restaurant clients.

Back in 2008, at the height of a recession, I received a message from a young man who said he and his father were looking to open a restaurant. I thought to myself, "Really, opening a restaurant in a recession?" Everyone was cutting back on eating out and other discretionary expenses, and restaurants were closing weekly.

I mentioned this to my business partner, who shook his head. But we had nothing to lose and were looking for more clients, so I called the young man back and set up a meeting.

Then we heard his story. He wanted to open a restaurant to honor the family's matriarch, who loved to entertain and welcome family and friends into her home. Their home was THE place where the kids hung out. We all have memories of such a place.

They had a vision, of creating that type of atmosphere, in a neighborhood setting where they would welcome locals and visitors alike and treat them like family. However, they were justifiably nervous about being able to hire and keep the right staff when everyone was job-hopping from one place to the next, chasing the dollar.

They were more than willing to pay a competitive wage, but in their hearts, they knew if they did not take a vested interest in their staff, particularly in a recession, they would likely end up like most of the other open restaurants—with a revolving door—or worse yet, following the other 50 percent of new restaurants that close in their first year.

While they asked themselves what this new restaurant would look and feel like and how to attract residents and visitors (the location was in a very popular urban beach community) to their restaurant, we decided to involve their interview candidates and the neighborhood residents.

You know what they received? They found a lot of input and respect. The candidates and eventual team members felt part of the process because they were.

Their staff took pride in their jobs. So, when they invited diners in—friends, family, and colleagues—the owners and waitstaff also asked for input on their menu, the food, and the service.

They then met with their staff and refined the dining experience, all before officially opening their doors. When they did, the guests came back, and the staff (for the most part) stayed—at least the ones the owners wanted to stay.

Even better, they were profitable. In their first year. In a RECES-SION. They had an 80 percent retention rate, which was actually 100 percent because the owners made the decision to ask the ones who did not fit to leave.

Now the best part is that these strategies apply to any type of business—not just restaurants.

This includes an insurance company owner whom I met at a referral and networking meeting shortly after he purchased a book of business from the previous owner. He came from an insurance background but had never owned a business before and wanted some leadership and sales training. He had two staff, both of whom were underperforming.

Through a profit acceleration assessment, we identified his barriers to profitability, including his staffing needs, which were not in line with his goals. By working on and developing his vision (what he wants to be known for) and his mission statements (what he and his team do every day to achieve the vision), he was able to identify the employee to keep and the employee to let go. Being a kindhearted man and employer, he kept giving his primary sales—yet underperforming—employee "just one more chance."

After speaking with this employee and setting some goals, she was still underperforming and causing him more angst, which also carried over to his other, higher-performing, staff person due to his own personal stress. After several discussions and realizing the primary salesperson was a limiting factor, he finally let her go.

Then the tables turned. His sales doubled in the first month after she left. He had more energy. He started doing what he loved—making sure people had the right, not just any, coverage (his vision) and sharing that with his other employee, who was responsible for policy renewals. We scripted her sales call sheet, allowing her to effectively reach out to existing clients and fill in their insurance gaps.

By focusing on and applying his vision of making sure people have the right insurance and doing what he loved (helping people)—and letting go of the person who did not see or share this vision—he became the #2 regional salesperson in his first six months in business.

Another client who owns a painting company came to me after working with another coach and seeing no results. He had a good referral base and solid contractor team but wanted to grow his business and differentiate himself in the marketplace. His goal was to double his business and contractor teams in 12 to 18 months in a very competitive and labor market. He was also weary of competitors luring away his crew. He wanted to know ways to retain them as well as attract new members (construction and painting being very volatile with employee turnover).

By applying the key strategies around vision and mission, he reduced his costs by 30 percent, kept his average contractor tenure to more than three years, and achieved 99 percent on-time performance for all of the company's projects.

The really good news is that **each of these owners spent less than three hours per week to achieve these goals.**

You may think this all takes a lot of time, but in fact, it just takes focus. Most of the work is accomplished in one weekly one-hour call, where we systematically review each step and document the process so there is a standard operating procedure to follow and refine as needed. With a foundational focus that starts with a company's vision, this proven process streamlines the hiring from the start and then is applied to existing team members to improve retention. Everyone is excited to grow the business because they are part of the team and the end result—more work, more money, more benefits.

Everyone experiences different results, but they all have specific factors in common—improved standard operating procedures, hiring and retention, and profitability.

While every business is unique, the principles behind sound marketing and what WORKS in attracting and keeping the right employees are the same. You are still the gatekeeper to the business, but when you give keys to your staff, you empower them to feel like they contribute and learn more. They become aligned with you because you are aligned with them.

CHAPTER TWO

—

The Roadmap
(aka training program)

DRAWING UPON my 15+ years as a running coach, I realized that what most CEOs and business owners lack is a personal roadmap—or training program—that systematically takes them from where they are to where they want to be. It's the same founding principles and process that became part of my own coaching and training, both as a marathon runner as well as a business owner.

This proven process can transport you from where you are today—possibly just getting off the couch or looking to run in a 10K, half marathon, or marathon—with a desired goal but frustrated, challenged, overwhelmed, and uncertain about the process to the finish line.

Hiring and retention are no different. There's uncertainty, concern about the time involved, and likely apprehension about whether you can or even want to do it, but something inside of you says, "I'd like to try because I don't like (fill in the blank), and I want to (fill in the blank)."

Your roadmap (or training program) starts with an assessment of where you are today and where you want to be by XXX. And then it's a step-by-step or day-by-day process. Looking at the end goal date and what it is, back it out 120 days and set a goal. And then the 30-day goal, and then 7 days, and then what you need to do today (one thing) to get you closer to achieving your goal. If you do one thing every day, that's 5 things in a week, 20 things in a month (factoring in weekends for time off to recharge), and 1,300 in a year (or let's adjust to 1,000 because life and vacation and family do come up—as they should).

And just one thing per day. It's called making your current challenge/goal (i.e., improving your hiring and retention) your top priority. People get overwhelmed because they make the little things the priority, staring at the to-do list, which in and of itself is negative because it's a "to do" instead of "a choose." When you decide to make your goal the priority and just one thing every day, that small incremental change turns into compounded growth, just like the one thing turns into over 1,000 in a year.

The pathway or roadmap is moving forward from where you are and breaking the goal down into pieces. Like a training plan, you can't skip to week four until you complete weeks one, two, and three. When it comes to retention (the end goal), you MUST start with hiring to make sure that you start on the right foot. It's much easier to progress through the training/hiring and retention process when you take it one step at a time and start from the beginning vs. trying to get to the end as quickly as possible.

Like training for a race or getting fit, you start seeing small, incremental changes that give you more confidence. You start to feel better. Your new hires become integrated into the program with your existing staff. Every week, you review your progress—what went right, where you can improve, or when to stay on plan if it's working. The key here is consistency.

Then, before you know it, you love your job more, see your profits grow, and oversee productive staff who are engaged and working toward a common goal (your vision).

If you're reading this book right now, it's because you still struggle with finding and keeping the right employees—the employees who matter.

You probably tried other options—courses, coaching, seminars, webinars, and books—and still are not finding the result you want. You have a sense of overwhelm wondering what to do. There's so much information out there, and the media and social platforms don't help.

There are tons of books and information about the importance of company culture and employee engagement. However, in all my research, I have yet to find a source that gives CEOs and business owners, such as yourself, a roadmap that guides them through the process and simplifies it in a way they can comprehend and say, "Wow, I could do this."

So, I am going to walk you through these steps so you, too, can move on and minimize the frustrations, concerns, and challenges you face around hiring and retention.

CHAPTER THREE

———

Where You Are

I EQUATE HIRING AND RETENTION to ordering a filet mignon and getting a hamburger. You think you deserve the best. You think you have done everything right. And yet you end up with a lesser product, compromising what you know in your heart you—and your business—deserve.

You're frustrated. You keep trying but don't see any end in sight.

You think it's all about the money, so you continue to raise wages and salaries, trying to compete with larger companies. Consequently, you feel like you can't afford benefits. You just need bodies in the door.

And guess what you get? You get bodies who are chasing the money, furthering your belief that it's all about the money. It has a trickle-down effect.

You feel like you're on a teeter-totter. You set up interviews, and they repeatedly don't show, or even call. Then you have what you think is a great interview, make an offer, and find out they accepted a position with someone else.

Now, you have a hard time filling shifts and the void for extra help, and your loyal staff become decreasingly unmotivated by burnout. You're at a loss for what to do. I know that feeling. I've been there.

You think you're doing everything right and still have a revolving door. You wonder if anyone really wants to work. You spend most of your time putting out fires, dealing with overhead, trying to appease customers and your staff, and thinking there is no end in sight. To make matters worse, the media keeps hyping on the "great resignation" and labor shortage.

All of this eats away at your profits, further affecting your mood, your confidence, and your ability to even think about *running* your business because you spend so much time *doing* your business to maintain operations and pay the bills.

You're overwhelmed. So, in an effort to act like you're trying, you take the same measures—raise wages and salaries and ask your existing staff to do more. You become increasingly resentful and find yourself with an eroding company culture.

You're not alone. Hiring challenges are the #1 frustration facing business owners and organization leaders today. I struggled with them too, running my PR and marketing firm. I loved every minute of my job, until the day a key employee quit.

I began to spiral out of control and put a barrier between myself and my business partner. We thought we were doing everything right, too. We gave her annual salary increases, let her handpick her clients, and shielded her from the other challenges we faced running a business.

To make matters worse, we later discovered that she left because she did not feel valued and appreciated. Ouch. We thought, "What else does she need?" Her leaving could not have come at a worse time. We were maxed out on client work.

We quickly hired someone—anyone—and this person eroded our company culture and nearly destroyed our business. I started worrying about the future, paying for college for my son, and covering mortgage payments and other increasing expenses. I felt like all I did was put out fires and manage overhead. I hated my job.

You may be wondering, "How could one person do that?"

I learned it wasn't about any single person. It was my reaction to external circumstances and the message I delivered after hiring the wrong person and then keeping them there. I wanted to be "fair" and give him a chance when, in my heart, I knew he was not the right fit. I was so afraid of not having the support, failing as a president and owner, that I kept doing the same thing and expecting a different outcome. As Albert Einstein has been credited, this is "the definition of insanity."

Our existing staff became increasingly resentful and, as a result, contributed to more and more business "fires." They were slacking off because they thought, "Why bother?"

It wasn't just happening to me. My clients experienced it too.

As business owners and CEOs, we are constantly faced with addressing challenges. Covid put this on steroids. But if you're here, you got through it. You found a way. You took an obstacle, adapted, and adjusted, even if it was hard.

Now you're back in business facing the next pandemic—the labor shortage.

You're tired. You just want things to be easier. You wish you could easily find people who want to come work for you. I hear it all the time: "Back in our day, we went to work and got a paycheck, and that was good enough. What happened to the work ethic?"

Yes, it has changed, but the work ethic has not gone away. It's just different. When you can embrace this and understand the three key strategies to attract the right employees—the ones who align with your vision—those interviews and offers turn into new team members, and the team members you have stay longer. Your profits also improve because everyone is aligned to a common goal.

CHAPTER FOUR

Why You Can't Afford to Stay Where You Are

Where you are NOW...

- Frustrated

- Doing the same thing and hoping for a different outcome

- Dealing with burnout (you AND your staff)

- Struggling to fill shifts/positions

- Waning customer/client satisfaction

- Increased overhead

- Diminishing profits

Where you CAN be...

- Happy staff

- Happy clients/customers (who bring you more business)

- Spending more time running (versus doing) your business

- Reduced turnover (up to 60 percent)

- Greater revenue streams (50 percent plus)

- Increased profits (70 percent plus)

- Increased work satisfaction

- Taking a vacation!

The question is... are you going to stay where you are, follow the pack, and make excuses for why you can't find or keep the employees who matter?

OR

Become the leader you were meant to be and seek the help you know you need so you can stand out as the business where the RIGHT people want to come to work—and stay?

It's not your fault. I didn't know either, but now that I do, I'm here to help you in the same way I found help.

So, who is this book for?

It is NOT for someone who...

- Thinks it's all about the money;
- Looks for a magic pill to resolve hiring and retention issues;
- Lacks passion for their business;
- Views staff as a cost, not an investment;
- Thinks everyone is lazy and doesn't want to work;
- Thinks they can't afford employee benefits;
- Wishes things would "get back to normal";

- Thinks they can figure it out on their own; and

- Doesn't want to change.

This book is for you IF you are the business owner or CEO who genuinely WANTS to:

- Attract and keep the employees who matter;

- Adopt more efficient and productive hiring and retention processes;

- Improve profits by reducing turnover;

- Be open to change, even with an unknown starting point;

- Embrace the value of INVESTING in yourself, your business, and your team;

- Discover a roadmap/training program to improve hiring, retention, and profits—FASTER; and

- Become THE place to work AND conduct business.

CHAPTER FIVE

―――

The Cost of Inaction

IF YOU'RE STILL NOT CONVINCED, let me explain the cost of inaction.

According to Workhuman,[1] employee turnover costs companies more than $1 trillion per year or 1.5 to 2 times the staff person's annual salary. Breaking this down, the average cost to replace an hourly employee is $1500, and 100-150 percent for a technical staff person. The turnover cost for C-Suite executives is 213 percent of their annual salary.

So, if you have 15 employees making minimum wage and a 33 percent turnover rate of 5 employees per year, that's $7500. Taking it to the next level, a company who has 15 employees that make $25/hour or $52K annual salary with a 25 percent turnover rate (four employees) costs $208,000 based on 100 percent of annual salary.

―――――――

1 "What Is the Cost of Employee Turnover? Is It High? | Workhuman," Workhuman, last modified October 11, 2023, https://www.workhuman.com/blog/the-ridiculously-high-cost-of-employee-turnover/.

And it gets worse... a company with 35 employees who loses 3 hourly employees at $18/hour, 1 technical person making $60,000/year, and one C-Suite executive making $175,000/year runs into a loss of $372,750. Ouch!

But this is just the surface. There are hidden costs too, such as advertising the position(s), training new hires, and recovering lost productivity.

Knowing there is likely to be some turnover every year, even a 50 percent reduction in your current turnover rate would keep more than $100K in your pocket. Do I have your attention now?

How would it feel if you could get at least 20 percent of your day back? How would it feel if you could reduce turnover even by 20 percent or 30 percent and see that money in your bank account? What if you could reduce your daily time investment in employee turnover, improve your retention by investing two to three hours per week, and implement a revamped hiring and retention program in three months or less? How would you feel with happier staff, where everyone looks forward to working with you to grow your business?

You don't have time to NOT address your turnover if you truly want to attract and keep the employees who matter. Down the street, there is a business owner or company already addressing these areas, and they are recruiting the team members you wish would come to you.

But wait. There's more!

According to The Muse,[2] a career development and search platform, and a February 2023 research study of 7,000 respondents, what is most important to job seekers today is work-life balance, with unhealthy, unsupportive work environments the primary culprit. To be sure, compensation is important, but overall, work-life balance outpaced compensation.

Overall, 70 percent of survey respondents said they evaluate a company's work-life balance to determine if it's a good fit for them, followed by 67 percent of respondents who ranked pay as the most important measure. Other factors workers consider in choosing an employer include:

- 59 percent — Learning and growth opportunities
- 59 percent — Office culture and colleagues' likability
- 58 percent — Job perks and benefits
- 47 percent — Job security
- 41 percent — Company leadership

I hear pushback all the time about not being able to afford benefits. Think about this. If you reduce your turnover by 20 or 30 percent and designate a portion of that to retaining your staff with the benefits THEY WANT, not the ones YOU WANT them to have—you have zeroed in on a point of differentiation in the hiring process (see Market-Dominating Hiring in Chapter 11) AND why they stay.

---

2 "2023 User Survey," 2023, TheMuse, accessed November 12, 2023, https://hire. themuse.com/rs/084-RRC-895/images/The_Muse_2023_White_Paper_4.17.pdf.

———

CHAPTER SIX

Common Objections

I HEAR ALL THE TIME, "These all sound well and good, but I don't have the time. I just need bodies in the door."

The reality is, though, that you receive what you put into the universe. If you think you don't have time, you don't. If you just need bodies in the door, you get those too. I understand. I felt this way, too, before.

I knew at a pretty young age I wanted to make a difference and stand out. My dad was a minister, so I was raised in a household with a give-back mentality. The downside was the message I learned: "Make enough to get by but not ahead."

My mother was a stay-at-home mom until my two older sisters were in high school, and college expenses were looming. As a music major in college with no real job experience, my dad found receptionist work for my mom at his office. Not completely satisfying or rewarding for her, she decided to volunteer and prove her worth to obtain paid positions.

By applying the skills she learned and her own tenacity in figuring out how to cook—all while managing a home and family with three kids on a limited budget—she worked her way into executive director and corporate management training positions. She was an amazing role model who demonstrated that I could do anything I put my mind to.

When my turn for college arrived, I had fallen in love with skiing. I took my mom's lead, discovered my own next best place, and found a way to make it work. This place was Colorado—at a private university—on a minister's salary. But I was passionate about skiing and found a college that gave me access and a communications program that appealed to me. I was given a budget of what my parents could afford and then told to "make up the difference."

So, I worked, including an internship at Colorado Ski Country USA, the trade association representing all the ski resorts in Colorado. After two weeks, I remember saying, "This is so much fun. I can't believe they would pay me to do it."

As I thought about my career, I realized I would spend more time working than anything else—including sleep, which I really love—so I'd better love what I do.

Fast forward 10 years and after amazing positions at Colorado Ski Country, the Colorado Tourism Board, and a private PR firm, there always came a time when I left. It came down to being frustrated with management styles, bureaucracy, no upward mobility, and ultimately, not feeling fully valued or respected.

I followed the path of 85 percent of most small business owners—I decided to bite the bullet, put my name on the door, and start my own firm. I loved every minute of it. As I said before, eventually, there came a time when I didn't, after I lost that key employee, and my business began to spiral. I hated my job, and I resented my staff, who I felt were entitled. I just wanted them to do the job and be grateful for a position. Our company culture eroded.

I thought, "How can I love what I do again?"

I merged my business with another larger agency that wanted to grow their PR division. I just wanted to return to client work, where I earned money and respect for what I brought to the table for this agency. Unfortunately, I ended up in a worse company culture than the one I had.

I was determined. There must be a better way. So, I jumped into the river (so to speak), left the larger agency, and began my mission of helping business owners and CEOs find their better ways—addressing their barriers to profitability—which today, is mostly centered around hiring and retention.

CHAPTER SEVEN

The Seven Biggest Mistakes

LOOKING BACK on my own history, as well as that of hundreds of other companies and businesses, I discovered the seven biggest mistakes most business owners and CEOs make (including yours truly). Probably not all at once but over the course of time, the following are the seven standouts.

Big Mistake #1: Using the "Great Resignation" as an Excuse for Not Changing

Brian Scott, one of my favorite mindset coaches, says, "It's not what's happening externally. It's our reaction to it."

Time and again, I see business owners and CEOs using what I call the new labor pandemic or great resignation as an excuse for not adapting to hiring and retention challenges. This became readily apparent during Covid, when I discovered two schools of thought or mindsets.

The "I cant's" use whatever is happening externally as an excuse for not moving forward because they didn't have to go to work, show up, or be accountable to anyone.

And then there are the "How Can I's?" who say, "OK, my gym is closed, so how can I still work out?" Suddenly, there was a boom in bike sales, outdoor fitness classes, and home gym equipment.

Yes, we can fall back on whatever the media tells us, or we can move into the "How Can I?" camp and find a solution, like the solution I bring you in this book. However, my solution will require you to change your way of thinking from "There is no one who wants to work" to "How can I find the right people who want to work and are a fit for my business?"

Big Mistake #2: Adopting a "Bodies in the Door" Hiring Method

Do your job ads look like this? If so, you are advertising for bodies, NOT people. Sometimes you may just need a body, but you're not building your company. You're just getting by and expecting a different result. When you just have bodies, how are your customers treated?

Big Mistake #3: Making it All About You and Your Business/Company

Sorry, it's NOT about you. It's about THEM. Ninety-Nine percent of companies and businesses talk about how great they are WITHOUT conveying how they understand the problems of their prospective employees, current staff, or customers and HOW they, as the business, can be the solution provider.

Big Mistake #4: Not Having or Sharing Your Vision

You may ask, "What does vision have to do with hiring and keeping employees?" A LOT. Your vision is what gets you up in the morning. It represents your and your team's contribution to the greater good. It aligns you AND your team with a shared vision. It allows you to screen potential employees to make sure they understand and share your vision. If not, then they're just a body or not a right fit.

Big Mistake #5: Not Understanding What Makes Employees (and Prospects) Feel Valued and Appreciated

It's NOT all about the money. Yes, a competitive wage is important, but if you pay a competitive wage, numerous studies including The Muse White Paper[3] and Indeed[4] show that work-life balance and feeling valued and respected are the top reasons people want to stay because there is the following:

- A shared vision, as well as its importance;

- A demonstrated understanding of what's important to THEM and a commitment to investing in them versus "paying" them; and

- A recognition of their value—acknowledging, asking for input, thanking, showing appreciation—individually and in team settings.

Big Mistake #6: Overlooking Your Greatest Marketing Asset—Your Team

When it comes to customer service, your team is your greatest asset. Not only in how they treat your customers but also in the information they gather through input, questions, and feedback that the customers give them. The better they feel about their position and where

---

3 Ibid.

4 Indeed Editorial Team, "16 Reasons Employees Leave Their Jobs," Indeed Career Guide, last modified July 31, 2023, https://www.indeed.com/career-advice/career-development/reasons-employees-leave.

they work and, most importantly, being recognized for the contribution they make, the more likely your customers are going to feel the same. You can do this by:

- Asking for their input on projects, programs, and services;

- Checking in with them on what they love about working at your business; AND

- What "WE" can improve upon;

- Having regular team meetings (weekly is best) and reviews (at least once per quarter);

- Taking advantage of exit interviews.

Big Mistake #7: Sabotaging Employee Growth—Without Even Knowing It

You are not transparent about the challenges you encounter while running a business. Perhaps you micromanage. Maybe you spend more time doing their job or telling them how to do it than allowing them to do it the way they see works best. Don't let your fear of failure keep you from embracing it as a way to learn and grow.

CHAPTER EIGHT

The Three Key Strategies

WHEN I DISCOVERED the three key strategies for success—along with what most CEOs and business owners do without even knowing it—they became game changers for my business, my clients, and other companies that follow these three principles.

They center around:

- Your vision;

- Your employees' perceived value and appreciation; and

- How you are sabotaging their growth without even knowing it.

It's not your fault. I didn't know either.

The good news is these strategies work for any business at any price point.

$500K
$1M
$5M and more...

I will share these three strategies with you in the same way I wish someone had shared them with me earlier in my career. I will show you how to make lemonade out of lemons.

You CAN attract the right employees, even in a labor shortage.
You CAN keep them longer.
You WILL improve your profits.
And you will ENJOY running your business again.

The best part is you can do all this WITHOUT spending more money on marketing or advertising, WITHOUT having to invest more than two to three hours per week, and WITHOUT having any HR experience.

These strategies align you and your business in the right way so that you can more effectively communicate the value you place on your prospective and current employees, which in turn makes you and your business more valuable to them.

It's no secret the hiring process is complex. But since you have a busy life and likely want answers sooner than later, we're going to focus on the three key strategies that really make a difference—and how they relate to hiring and retention.

Vision
Mission
Market-Dominating Hiring

Now, a lot has been written about employee engagement and company culture, but what it lacks is a clear process—a roadmap or training program per se—to set you on the right track. I call this market-dominating hiring. By developing and employing these key strategies, you CAN transform your hiring and retention to attract and keep the employees who matter.

So, I ask you, is the labor pandemic or "great resignation" your obstacle or your opportunity?

I'd like to show you how you can make the labor pandemic your opportunity and have your company be the place where people want to work—and stay.

CHAPTER NINE

Creating Your Vision

I BROUGHT UP EARLIER what a company's vision has to do with hiring and retention. The answer is everything. Your vision sets you apart from everyone else. It represents your reason for being and what you want to be known for. It's what gets you up every day and keeps you going because it goes beyond the day-to-day tasks that take their toll on all of us.

Most importantly, your vision is the key to making the right—and hard—decisions faster. It's the glue that holds your team together, allows you to filter through the résumés and interviews, and sets the expectation of what you want your business to achieve. Without a vision, there is no sense of purpose or belonging—two key components of attracting and keeping the employees who matter.

I discovered that it ALL starts with your vision. When I lost sight of my vision running my seven-figure PR and marketing firm as the company that delivers value on every level, I ended up focusing on everything I didn't like about my job. It took a merger and several years for me to realize that when you have vision, you have purpose. And it brings energy to you—and your team—every day.

With a clear, shared vision, you can use it to ENGAGE your employees and prospects and EMPOWER them on a day-to-day basis so you can go back to doing WHAT YOU LOVE—running your business versus doing your business.

And it hasn't just worked for me. It has helped thousands of business owners and CEOs effectively learn how to attract and keep the employees who matter and turn greater profits using these very strategies.

Your vision statement is YOUR—AND YOUR TEAM'S—united front on how to contribute to the greater good. It's like a concrete pour versus a house built on stilts for your business.

A vision and the corresponding mission statement/core values are the cornerstones for hiring—and firing. I lost sight of this when I started taking our staff for granted, and it cost me a key employee and eroded our company culture.

Not realizing the mistakes I made that compounded themselves into resenting my staff and my work, I sought the help of a business coach. Together, we pinpointed the three key areas I needed to address. When I did, it turned my business and ultimately my clients' businesses around, getting us off a house built on stilts to one with a concrete foundation.

While there are a multitude of descriptions on how to create your vision statement—or if you have one, how to refine it—there is one steadfast rule. Less is more.

Now, when I say less, I don't mean some kind of lukewarm, half-hearted phrase. I mean chunking it down so that it rolls off your lips. It becomes part of you. It is the foundation for the culture you want to have and share with your team, your clients, and your customers. Consider ten words or less. Pull it from your heart. Think about what really matters to you and how you want to define your business and the work you do.

When you think about your business, why did you start it or buy it? (Note that according to a study conducted by LivePlan,[5] the top reasons people start their own business are to pursue a passion, do it better than anyone else, create generational wealth, and support community efforts).

What kind of difference did you think, want, or believe you could create?

Are you living/practicing it now?

Be honest with yourself. It's not about getting it right or wrong. It's about making sure you have a purpose beyond the tasks associated with your business to keep you going. You want to engage yourself and your team every day. Notice I say every day. Some businesses have it on every team member's desktop. Some display it in the reception area as people enter an office. Most importantly, it should be something you revisit regularly with your team.

---

5 Wirth, Kody, "7 Real Reasons Why Entrepreneurs Start Their Own Business — LivePlan," LivePlan Blog, last modified April 5, 2022, https://www.liveplan.com/blog/reasons-why-entrepreneurs-start-businesses/.

BREAK THROUGH YOUR HIRING AND RETENTION BARRIERS

So, grab a piece of paper or your laptop and start jotting down words or phrases that are important to you about your business.

When you think about your business, what kind of difference do you want to make?

What do you want to be known for?

What do you want people to say about you and your business?

When I began this process with one of my insurance clients, I asked him what he did better than anyone else selling insurance. He replied, "I do the same thing as everyone else."

I said, "This is the last time you will ever say that."

Why? If you are just like everyone else, you do not offer anything special. You have no point of differentiation, not to your prospects, your employees, your customers/clients, and—most importantly—yourself. Having a vision unique to who you are, who you want to be, and what you want to be known for sets you apart. It makes you stand out because you have a reason for being, doing, and leading every day.

In working with this client, I started asking him questions about why he bought his insurance agency. He responded, "To have something I own and more independence. I would actually like to own several businesses and just manage them and have them make me money." I then asked him why this was important to him. "I would like to spend more time with my kids and play games."

Next, I asked him why he pursued the insurance business. "It's something I have some experience in, and I've never owned a business. This seemed to make sense. I discovered I could buy a book of business that had a good track record and start out running." With this focus in mind, it didn't take long to find that business, so he made an offer that fit his budget.

Still not reaching a true vision, I dug a little deeper. Why insurance? He said, "Because I want to make sure people have the right insurance, whether they buy from me or not."

And there we had it—his vision—to make sure people had the right insurance (regardless from whom they bought it). It fit all the key hot buttons that would allow him to approach his existing client base (the first place any business owner should start as it costs at least three times more to recruit a new client than more business from an existing one) and look for gaps in their coverage.

His vision also helped us develop a call script for his remaining assistant, who is responsible for policy renewals. He met with her and shared his vision (and mission statements—more on that in the next chapter) and asked for her input on processes they can employ every day to make sure people have the right—not just any—insurance. They agreed for her to look at every policy coming up for a renewal and find any potential gaps in coverage.

When making the renewal policy follow-up calls (note that she is calling these people first, not emailing them), she noted that "we" (adopting the team approach) noticed we are covering XXX but not XXX. Then she stated the vision statement, "We're asking about this as it's important to us to make sure all our clients have the right insurance, not just any insurance." This took all the "cold" out of calling, as it came from a place of compassion and caring.

And you know what happened? Sales doubled. We focused on his vision, shared it, involved his team, and started filling in the gaps. Profits grew.

This approach also helped another chiropractor client who wanted to grow his business. He had a very good reputation for helping patients who thought there was no hope. When starting his vision process, he said he wanted to be their first resource—not their last— and serve as the trusted place where patients could come and find solutions to their health and daily wellbeing challenges.

I asked him, "What would that look like?" He said it would be about developing a referral network that worked both ways. If he couldn't help them, he could recommend them to others who "filled his gaps" and vice versa. So, we used this as his concrete pour and started branding every component of his business from this vision.

You can do this on your own or have someone work with you. I find it helps to have an outside person or a coach help you. They have a unique ability to know the right questions to ask, help you articulate your vision, and then cull it down to one simple sentence.

When done right, your vision should completely resonate with you. I call it the goosebump effect. It's living your true nature and purpose so that, when you think about it, you say to yourself, "If I did this, I would make a real difference and be known for making that difference." It's like the best testimonial a client or customer could write.

One of the best pieces of advice I ever received early in my PR career was when I worked at Colorado Ski Country USA and hosted media parties to promote Colorado as a ski destination. I was talking with a prominent ski resort PR Director as the media arrived. I saw him glance across the room, and he politely excused himself and walked over to a middle-aged man. Later that evening, I mentioned this to him and asked who he was, assuming he was someone "important." He said he was a writer for a small newspaper. I was curious, thinking he was an important editor. "Holly, it's not about how you treat the big editors. It's how you treat the small ones," he said. "You will always be remembered by how you treat the small people, not how you treat the big ones."

When I started my first PR and marketing firm and considered what I wanted it to be known for, I knew I wanted it to be viewed as something larger than myself, even if it never became more than just me. I wanted to think big, act big, feel big, and make my clients and the media feel that way too. While it wasn't a vision statement per se, it was a feeling I wanted to foster—to make everyone feel valued and important—as a PR person, business owner, and boss.

And you know what happened? I became that. My firm became "big" in the PR hospitality travel and tourism PR world. In six months, I had a dream-worthy client list. We didn't have big national accounts, but we had important ones—representing the kind of restaurants, hotels, destinations, and experiences on must-visit or bucket lists. Everyone was important and "big" in how we treated them as a client or media person, as well as internally on our team. We all had an important role to play. Everyone felt valued and respected. We set ourselves apart by doing really good work, caring, and attending to all of the little details.

How do you relate and make people feel important? Do you pay equal attention to the younger/less experienced staff as to your more seasoned managers? What about your customers? Are they treated equally or given preferential treatment? How do you inherently feel about them and believe they should be treated?

It all starts with your mindset. If you inherently believe people do not deserve to be treated equally or at least given the opportunity to shine—and make mistakes—you will struggle with attracting and keeping the right employees—and customers or clients.

A simple mindset shift can make a huge difference. This is where your vision comes into play. You get buy-in from the get-go. If you don't, the interview is over, and you move on.

"But that takes time, more time than I have." Sound like you?

How much time do you want to continue putting into interviews and hiring people just to get bodies in the door versus "taking the time" to make sure you recruit the right employees? You can attract them, but you need to engage them, not just hire them.

So, I'll ask you again. When you think about your business, why did you start it or buy it? What kind of difference did you think, want, or believe you could make?

How often do you think about this? Do you share it with your prospects and team members? Do they even know what your vision is?

———

CHAPTER TEN

Fulfilling Your Vision Through Mission Statements

ONCE YOU HAVE your vision in place, the next important step is to create your mission—the specific actions you and your team take every day to achieve your vision.

Your mission comprises a series of statements, ones that you as the business owner outline and then share with your team. Then, you should ask for their input. If you haven't shared your vision (or modified it), this is the time to get buy-in and then ask, "Given our vision, what do we need to do every day to achieve this?" (Note the usage of "our" and "we).

Let's assume your vision is to become the #1 place to work in your region. What do you need to do every day to become this?

Mission statement examples could include:

- We implement best hiring practices by writing compelling job descriptions, centered around sharing information on our vision, who we are, the characteristics and qualities of our ideal candidates, and then the responsibilities for each position.

- We make sure we have buy-in on our vision from all prospects and team members.

- We value and respect every prospect and team member by asking for their input.

- We conduct weekly team meetings to review goals, priorities, and responsibilities.

- We celebrate the successes and allow for mistakes (and learn from them).

- We regularly recognize people for their contributions and good work.

- We openly share and communicate goals and projected outcomes.

- We keep everyone informed on challenges we face as a business and with our clients/customers as a learning opportunity for everyone.

- We view every position as a career path and seek ways to help everyone learn and grow.

- We seek to promote from within first.

- We view every team member as a valued contributor to the success of our business.

You should approach your team and say, "I have this goal/vision of becoming the #1 best place to work in the region, and I would appreciate your input on what we do best and what we can improve upon."

You always want to start with the successes. It's a safer (and kinder) place for people to provide input and start to feel trusted and valued. Go through the mission statement list one by one and ask for their input on a scale of 1 to 10. Ask, "How good are we at doing this?"

How can we do it better? What else should we be doing? What are the challenges we face or get in the way of achieving agreed-upon goals? What kind of support do you, as team members, need to perform your job better? Like your job more? Love your job?

Do not be afraid to ask. You can assume, or you can ask for their opinions and vastly improve your retention.

Whether your vision is to be the #1 best place to work or serve as the solutions provider for your clients/customers, the process is the same. What's key is that your mission statements involve your team members, and you visit them regularly to update, refine, or improve.

Remember my insurance client? His business and sales started to grow after he let go of the underperforming salesperson and made his remaining assistant part of the process versus telling her what to do. He also explained why it was important. These measures gave him a solid foundation from which to grow his business and connect with his clients, ask about their current insurance, offer to review policies without any obligation, and make recommendations.

Most importantly, it worked because his vision and corresponding mission statements were aligned with who he is and the kind of business he wants to run and be known for—and what brings him joy in his work. These also help motivate him and his assistant/team and mitigate frustration and anxiety around "cold calling."

Let me explain.

Think about it. Is there any part of "cold calling" that sounds appealing and makes you want to jump out of bed each morning because you're "so excited to make all those cold calls today?" How do you think it makes your salespeople feel?

When you focus on how calls help you get closer to your vision, as well as how you can make the process more fun, rewarding, and gratifying, you greatly increase buy-in. Then ask what they need to better do their job and, most importantly, enjoy it more. This is where getting buy-in from the get-go is important, so expectations are clear. The more specific, the better.

Remember, you are not looking for a body. You are looking for team members who want to learn, grow, improve skillsets, and contribute to a business they believe in.

One of my own coaches once told me, "Holly, if you don't let people and organizations know about what you do and how you can help them, you are doing a disservice to everyone." Have you ever conveyed this to your team?

I'm not saying calls aren't important—they are. According to Jeb Blount, author of *Fanatical Prospecting,* his own research noted in the book demonstrated that personal calls outperform social media

3:1 when done effectively. But stop referring to them as cold calls. Find ways to make them "warm," like my insurance client. Work with your team on how to implement this change… and then shut up. Wait for them to respond. Listen—really listen. What are they saying?

Here is your opportunity to lead—to run your business versus do your business. This is how you lead from your vision, which should come from your heart. If it's all about money, you may find success, but it won't last. It's not a concrete foundation. It's a house built on stilts.

This also applies to your clients, customers, and team members. When you involve them in the process and discussion, they feel valued and appreciated. Then it's up to you to keep them informed and demonstrate, not just in words but also with actions, the steps you are taking to implement some of their recommendations and explain why you are not adopting others.

This is not about giving up control or being manipulated into taking actions that don't make sound sense financially. It's about engaging your team members, asking for their input, and then using this intel to make decisions in the best interest of your business.

CHAPTER ELEVEN

Market-Dominating Hiring

NOW THAT YOU HAVE POURED the concrete with your vision and mission statements, it's time to start building your house. Start with getting inside the heads of your employee prospects, which I call your market-dominating messaging, the foundation for market-dominating hiring. It's a conversion formula that helps you trump your competitors.

Simply put, getting inside of the heads of your employee prospects comes down to addressing the number one question in their minds.

The conversion formula works like this:

- INTERRUPT—the problem(s) your employee prospects have and don't want;

- ENGAGE—the solution they want but don't have;

- EDUCATE—how you, as the employer, demonstrate your ability to become the prospect's solution provider; and

- OFFER—what they can't refuse (hint: it's not all about the money. If it is, they are not your right candidate).

Like any formula or equation, you need to address all the parts, not just a few.

You may ask, "How do I know what their problems are? I just need bodies in the door. I don't have time for this, nor can I afford it."

Yes, you may be able to get bodies in the door, but they're just bodies. They don't stay. They view what they do as a job, not a career. Every position in your business/company should be viewed as a career path position. If it's just a job, you and your business will experience the same revolving door you have had for the past few—if not more—years.

I can hear it now, "Most of our positions ARE jobs—hourly wage employees who are just looking for a job."

Let's do a little reverse psychology. What if you took the 30-foot view of every position in your business? Look at each one as a career opportunity—a stepping stone to another position and/or a set of skills they can learn that they can use and apply to future positions, or just life in general. What if you took the view as a leader to find ways to help them learn and grow?

Do you ask your prospects/employees where they want to be in a year? Three years? What can you do to support them? How much effort do you put into finding out what they want versus assuming you know? Do you assume they are only in it for the money and will leave as soon as something better comes along?

To help you determine the top "problems" among prospective or even existing employees, consider the top reasons people stay—or leave—an organization.

Top Reasons Employees Left a Job in 2022[6]

1. Needing more of a challenge

2. Looking for a higher salary

3. Feeling uninspired

4. Wanting to feel valued

5. Seeking a better management relationship

6. Searching for job growth and career advancement

7. Needing more feedback or structure

8. Wanting a different work environment (it's not just about working from home)

9. Looking to live somewhere else

10. Feeling conflicted with workplace policies

11. Thinking their job has changed

12. Wanting a clearer company vision

13. Needing a better work-life balance

14. Seeking a more financially secure company

15. Wanting more independence

16. Looking for more recognition

---

6 Ibid.

Note that, aside from looking to live somewhere else and seeking remote work, each one of these is within your control. Now, offering a higher salary may seem out of your reach, but when you factor in the cost of turnover, it may cost you less to offer an increase and possibly some additional benefits that can still work within your bottom line.

Looking at these reasons, how do you think your business stacks up? Do you even want to know?

Be honest with yourself. If you are truly committed to "doing things right," you can turn the tables on your hiring and retention. And I will show you how.

Step 1:

Take the top reasons why employees left in 2022 and present them to your team. Do so over lunch in your conference room (let everyone order from a delivery menu, so they get what they want, not what is easy and convenient for you). Explain this is an open forum, and discuss your frustrations, concerns, and challenges. Show some vulnerability. Explain that you are committed to making your business the #1 place to work. To do this, you need their help and—most importantly—their input. Then hit the pause button.

Look around the room at their faces and body positions. Are they curious? Skeptical? Uncertain? Are they smiling?

Then ask for input. Pick out a skeptic. "<Name,> what are you thinking?" Let him/her/them know it's OK to voice their opinions. Explain you may not implement everything, but you need a starting point. It all begins with them—your most valuable asset.

Step 2:

Start with the positive. What do we do well as a company? You can use the top reasons people leave as a starting point and ask each staff person to rate your business on a scale of 1 to 5. Assure them there are no right or wrong answers and no one will get fired. Don't include names on the sheets. Have them collected into a folder so they remain anonymous. Use the same color pens. Then leave the room and appoint someone to collect the responses (seek out a facilitator if you prefer). You are not perfect, and leaders are aware of and accept their shortcomings and know when to bring someone in.

Note: Do NOT do this as an employee survey. Do it in person. No one needs more emails and, consciously or unconsciously, they will use it as an excuse. Then you're right back at spending too much time (and/or money) chasing people down. You really need the ones who are hesitant. This is not about receiving affirmation (though it doesn't hurt). It's about genuinely WANTING to know. Let them know that.

Step 3:

Tally the results. Try to look at this objectively. It's OK if it stings a little—or a lot. Remember, this is about genuinely WANTING to know how you can improve SO you can. If all you do is sit around, assuming and doing the same things, you will yield the same results.

Step 4:

Rally your team over coffee and some snacks (sharing food is a great icebreaker and gives people something to do) and go over the results. Acknowledge your appreciation in a genuine way. Then ask them for their input on the ranking results.

Start with the positive ratings first. What are we doing right? What would make X better? Then migrate into the lower ratings. How can we improve? What would get us from an X rating to a 5-star rating?

Listen. Take notes (or have a facilitator or HR person present to keep a record). Most importantly, DO NOT push this onto an outside survey company. For your team to trust you—the key ingredient here—they need to hear, and see, you as a critical part of the process.

If you're not comfortable with this, then this is where coaching would help. You MUST commit to change. It's supposed to be uncomfortable. If change was easy, everyone would do it. Ask yourself: are you REALLY willing to change? Be honest. It's the same with anything in life—losing weight, changing your diet, improving your marriage/relationships, etc. You have to be willing to face some truths so you can move forward.

CHAPTER TWELVE

Empowerment

YOUR EMPLOYEES are your greatest marketing tool. Their level of satisfaction is directly linked to your customers'/clients' level of satisfaction. Think about your current team and their average level of satisfaction. According to myperfectresume.com,[7] 74 percent of employees believe their workplace culture drastically influences how satisfied they are with their jobs and that workplace relationships account for 86 percent of employees' job satisfaction.

Look at your customer satisfaction. Does it mirror your employees? Do you even know? Do you even want to know?

This brings me to the next question. Do you view your employees as staff, employees, or a team?

---

7 Hanna, Kelly, "Job Satisfaction: Cracking the Job Happiness Code (Study)," My Perfect Resume, last modified June 5, 2023, https://www.myperfectresume.com/career-center/special-reports/job-satisfaction.

You may not think it's a big deal, but think about it. Who wants to be called into a "staff meeting?" It's like being called into the principal's office. But a "team meeting?" It's like you're all in this together.

The team meeting is where you share your vision, present mission statements (as a draft), and ask for their input.

Why does this matter? Because highly aligned organizations grow revenue 58 percent faster and are 72 percent more profitable, while significantly outperforming their unaligned peers in terms of engaging employees, retaining and satisfying customers, and effectively leading.[8]

This is PROVEN. But you must be willing to change and adapt. It does not have to cost you a lot of money or time. You just need a roadmap, like a training program, and a reasonable timeline to achieve it. You can't jump to the finish line of hiring until you have taken each step—one day, one week, one month—at a time to train or (change to your) body and your brain to reach the finish line.

Yes, you may be able to walk your way to a 5K finish, but wouldn't you rather run and get there faster? That takes training. Otherwise, it's just the same you, walking and wishing for a different outcome. Hey, it's OK if that's all you want, but don't pretend like you want to change. Just accept that you will continue to struggle and feel frustrated by turnover and lack of employee commitment.

---

8 "Organizational Alignment Research Model," LSA Global, accessed November 12, 2023, https://lsaglobal.com/insights/proprietary-methodology/lsa-3x-organizational-alignment-model/.

There is no going back to the way things were. You CAN thrive IF you make a shift in your hiring and retention practices—and most importantly your mindset.

You MUST be willing to do things differently. You don't need to do a lot. Small, incremental changes lead to compounded growth. If I told you that making some simple and consistent shifts could add upwards of 40 percent or more to your bottom line, would you be willing to change? My guess is you would say, "Heck, yes!"

Then there is the million-dollar question. Do you genuinely believe your team deserves more respect and appreciation—and your time—or are you doing this because of the money? If it's the latter, I'm sorry to say it won't work—or at least not the way you hope.

You MUST believe in the greater good. If you pretend you care and you still really believe the majority of people are lazy and don't want to work, it will only backfire and cause you more angst. So, be honest with yourself.

If it's only about the money, then you will have a business built on stilts and one that will crumble over time. Maybe not completely, but you will remain a victim of external influences. All the excuses in the world won't change the fact that if you don't genuinely want to train, support, and grow your team, your business will continue to operate—or struggle—in the same frustrating manner you face today.

It's like refueling your car or your body. You have to perform regular maintenance, hopefully before you run out of gas or energy, or the car—and you—will cease to run.

Alternatively, you can accept that times have—and will continue—to change, and you and your business are going to be the ones standing and thriving because you made the commitment to lay a concrete foundation. You truly believe and embrace that having the right hiring and retention practices are the building blocks for future growth and opportunity.

It really comes down to these three strategies—creating your vision, developing your mission statements, and market-dominating positioning. These can be your game changers to ATTRACT the right staff, keep them longer, and grow your profits.

I want you and your business or company to be the next best place to work. I want you to reduce your turnover by up to 60 percent and improve your bottom line by 70 percent or more. Are you game?

CHAPTER THIRTEEN

Attracting the *Right* Candidates

NOW THAT YOU'RE SET UP to succeed with your vision, mission statements, and market-dominating hiring practices in place, including buy-in from your team, it's time to craft a market-dominating hiring job description.

Remember, just like your ideal prospects, you want to stand out— NOT blend in. Say goodbye to generic job descriptions that apply to any business. You attract what you put out, and that includes sharing details about your business, character traits (before qualifications), the position, and ways to apply.

These specific details allow you to pre-qualify people—which is the goal—so that the résumés and applications you receive are worth your time to review. Yes, you will receive fewer résumés. But like leads, do you want a bunch of unqualified, unfitting people, or are you ready for quality over quantity?

Even if you "just need bodies," think about how time-wasting, angst-producing, and culture-killing it is to hire the wrong people. If you're in a pinch, how about offering some incentives for your existing team to participate? Remember to ASK them what they want—it may be pay, but it may be more vacation time. Time or money are typically the biggest motivators, outside of being asked instead of told.

Incorporate your vision into your job descriptions. You are looking for the ideal candidate, not just anyone, so the more specific you can be, the more likely this person will emerge. Also, other important elements for your job descriptions include:

- Your logo/brand at the top of the page (I can't tell you how many descriptions I have seen that have zero brand recognition);

- Position title;

- Start date;

- Company vision statement, general history, and how you achieve results for your customers/clients, and your points of differentiation;

- Character qualities you seek (this is different from qualifications);

- Qualifications, such as college/advanced degrees, years' experience, etc. (be candid in stating what you want and need);

- Details about the position, such as atmosphere, culture, work days/hours, remote/in-office/hybrid, vacation time, personal time, benefits, growth opportunities, salary, and other compensation/bonus opportunities;

- Ways to apply, such as whether you require a cover letter, or get creative by requesting a video in a specified amount of time to learn why candidates think they are a fit for your company. Be sure to include the email to send résumés. Ensuring they are willing to take the extra step filters the list to the employees you want—not the ones who just want an easy way out!; and

- The company website.

I recommend posting on more than one site. Google the best job search sites for your industry. There are many sites specific to career categories. I recommend at least one of these and another more far-reaching one, like Indeed. Be sure to also be geographically specific if needed for the position. If remote, cast a wider net.

Be patient. Quality takes time. Do you want it fast, or do you want it right? I know you want both. But remember how much that turnover costs you—tens, if not hundreds, of thousands of dollars, not to mention your time (40 percent of your day, every day). Do it right, and you will be rewarded.

CHAPTER FOURTEEN

———

The Interview Process

As with the job description, the goal of the interview process is to cultivate the details and the important questions that are also aligned with your organization. You are trying to find the right candidate, someone who is willing to be candid about their strengths and admit their weaknesses.

Avoid looking for perfection. I fell prey to this when interviewing for a mid-level account manager. She hit all the right notes. I never had such a great interview, and she turned out to be a nightmare hire. Be careful of people who are too perfect. Dig deep. Keep prompting, "Tell me more." Have them cite specific experiences and situations for each of the character qualities (or your top five), even for lower-level positions. As the saying goes, hire for character and train for skill.

How you treat lower-level team members is commensurate to what you will get in return. You are hiring career people, not people looking for a job, at every level.

Now, I want to recommend a simple, four-step interview process. Depending on the size of your organization and if you have a Board of Directors or HR person who needs to be involved, make sure they are on board with this process. You must be involved too. It's a top-down approach. If you remove yourself from the hiring equation, then it's just false promises that you actually care, and it WILL have a trickle-down effect.

This is your opportunity to shine as a leader and demonstrate that your team is the most important part of your and your organization's success. You might even learn from some valuable feedback on your vision. Trust me, you will stand out as a company that operates differently (in the right way) simply by being involved as the business owner, CEO, or organization leader.

You are trying to do the unexpected, and it will separate you from your competition.

Here are some key elements you should implement to maximize the value, impact, and success of each interview:

- All interviews should be done via Zoom or in person (for secondary interviews).

- Set parameters for every call by thanking them for their time and indicating how much time you allocated. Ask if that works for them.

- Always start with a positive remark to break the ice. For example, ask them about something that happened to them in the past week, what they did over the weekend, etc.

- If you are not sure what to ask, always default to "Tell me more." Referred to as going seven layers deep, you are trying to discover who they are and what motivates them.

1st "Discovery Call" Interview (15 minutes – this is just an initial screening)

Before the call, highlight a piece of information from their cover letter/résumé that caught your attention and ask them to tell you more about it.

Acknowledge your appreciation for them taking the time to meet with you. Then share your vision statement and that part of the company culture is obtaining input from the team.

Ask them, "If this was your company vision, what would you recommend we do every day to make sure we achieve this goal?"

Note: If all they do is reiterate what you said in the job description, the interview is over. They are not an open thinker. It's OK if they cite some key points from the description, but if that's all they do, they are not a fit.

If you like them and want to give them another opportunity—people are nervous—acknowledge that they basically repeated the job description back to you (i.e., you do pay attention). But there's always room for improvement. You could ask, "Is there anything you think we should be doing or could do?"

2nd Interview (schedule 30 minutes but plan on an hour)

Focus on character

What motivates them to work hard?

Go through the list of character traits and ask the candidate, on a scale of 1 to 5, with 5 being excellent, how would they rate themselves?

Take notes, and then ask them, "When I call your past employer or other references, how do you think will they rate you on each of these character traits?"

Watch their body posture and eyes. Shifting posture and eye contact indicates nervousness. If you sense this, offer them the opportunity to redo their personal rankings. Say, "We're about honesty and integrity. We're not looking for perfection."

If you want the interview to continue, review the time—see if you're getting close to the half hour—and ask how they are on time as you'd like to continue and ask a few more questions (they should have allocated more time—if not, that's a red flag).

Identify five of your most important character traits highlighted or ones that had different degrees of rating and ask them to give you an example of how they demonstrated each of these character traits in specific work/life examples.

Ask, "When I call your last employer or references, would they concur with you?"

If the interview is going well and you have time, continue with more questions, such as:

- Why are they passionate about <your industry>? Is there a personal story that aligns them even more with your industry (bonus as it's personal for them—career versus job)

- What gets them excited about working in your industry? Ask them to share a story.

3rd interview (or 2nd depending on how you feel about the candidate and timing) – 1 to 1.5 hours (depending on the position)

Focus on leadership (higher-level positions) and the candidate's ability to resolve issues, address challenges, and be a team player (all levels)

Where would they like to be in a year? Three years? Five years? What are they most passionate about with regard to the position?

How do they deal with emotionally charged/demanding clients/customers (always ask for an example of a challenging situation they handled)?

If compensation is tied to sales and bringing in new clients/customers, ask them how they feel about that. Have they worked in this business model before? What is their track record (you're looking for measurable, bottom-line results, not how many calls they made each day)? What do they love most about sales? Least?

How do they deal with a day when they lack motivation and uncertainty to make the calls, visits, etc.?

Discuss conflict resolution. Request they share a story about a challenging situation with a colleague and how they handled it. On a scale of 1 to 10, how do they feel they did? Would a colleague agree? Why or why not? What would they do differently?

Then ask the same question about a challenging situation with a client or customer.

Before the end of this call, raise the topic of compensation, benefits and ask for references.

3rd or 4th interview (1 to 1.5 hours)

Once you narrow the list to the top two or three candidates, get out of the way. Let your team know that you narrowed the field and are excited to have found someone(s) that you/the board believes is a good fit. Now, you would like their input.

Set up a time for the candidate(s) to meet with the team (or a handful from different positions if a larger company), without you. Pay for them to go out to lunch, out of the office.

You can also bring in an outside source (a coach or another colleague whom you trust and believe is a good read of people) to ask for their candid feedback.

When you're ready, make the offer, and include a weekly, monthly, and three-month review. You need to make sure you are visible and find the opportunity to check in and receive feedback. It's also important that you appoint a team member for this person to shadow, particularly the first week.

The key to your hiring and retention success is with you. Yes, it takes time. But it also gives you the opportunity to check in and make sure you and your team create the kind of company, business, or organization that stands out—from the inside out.

Bonus Offer

Thank you for purchasing your copy of *Break Through Your Hiring & Retention Barriers*. Although I highly recommend reading the book, I also understand we live in a fast world where video and audio options are also appreciated.

For this reason, I have created an on-line course where I cover this book in video, which can also be listened to in your car or on your phone in audio. Here, I share the key elements of this book and some additional insights.

To access this, please scan the QR code below:

Most importantly, thank you for reading my book. I hope you found some valuable insights and takeaways to improve your hiring and retention and greatly appreciate your feedback by posting a review here: HollyJohnsonBook.com/review
or by scanning the QR Code below:

I truly wish you all the best of luck and success in your personal and professional pursuits.